Intrinsic Desires

Brandon Gene Petit

authorHOUSE™
1663 LIBERTY DRIVE, SUITE 200
BLOOMINGTON, INDIANA 47403
(800) 839-8640
WWW.AUTHORHOUSE.COM

AuthorHouse™ *AuthorHouse*™ *UK Ltd.*
1663 Liberty Drive, Suite 200 *500 Avebury Boulevard*
Bloomington, IN 47403 *Central Milton Keynes, MK9 2BE*
www.authorhouse.com *www.authorhouse.co.uk*
Phone: 1-800-839-8640 *Phone: 08001974150*

©2007 Brandon Gene Petit. All rights reserved.

No part of this book may be reproduced, stored in a retrieval system, or transmitted by any means without the written permission of the author.

First published by AuthorHouse 2/6/2007

ISBN: 978-1-4259-8822-7 (e)
ISBN: 1-4208-9199-5 (sc)

Library of Congress Control Number: 2005909159

Printed in the United States of America
Bloomington, Indiana

This book is printed on acid-free paper.

Table of Contents

Origins 1
The unwritten quest 2
The call 3
Transience 4
Paroxysm 6
Urban storm 7
Scrolls 8
The early hours 9
Vestige 10
Intrinsic desires 11
Lupus 12
A universe in solitude 13
Two 14
Pathos 16
Temptress 17
Regression 18
Within and without 20
Spectacle 21
Fleeting 22
Want 23
For all eternity 24
Clove cemetery 25
Alterations 26
A dying breed 27
Let me in 28
Seeking sanctuary 29
Under lock and key 30
Whole 31
Beyond summer 32
Vomica 34
Elsewhere 36
Tooth and nail 38
People of the fog 39
My ghost walks 40
Ignis fatuus 41
Only human 43
Parted ways 45
De novo 46
Idle hands 48
Things to come 49
Still there 50
Disenchanted 51

Withdrawn	52
Theophobia	**54**
Plenty of time	55
The art of forgetting	**56**
The fifth column	57
Gray	**59**
In stride with giants	61
Doors and hallways	**62**
Misanthrope	64
Her	**65**
The touch of Eros	67
Look down	**69**
Diem ex die	70
The intercession	**72**
Epitomes	73
Deeper still	**74**
Evening eyes	76
Bring you to life	**77**
Circa 1988	78
Cruentus	**80**
Fever dreams	81
Matris	**82**
Words alone	83
Listen	**84**
The sensorium	86
Noctivagus	**88**
Away	89
The cycle	**90**
Alignment	92
Infitialis	**93**
Skyward	94
Odd folk	**95**
The final stretch	96
At an end	**98**

Origins

Haunting echoes of a distant chaos
The voice of past creations now lost
Reshape into forms that feed one another
The ripples in time that forever make path

The fluids of life now calmly circulating
Opposing forces contained in balance
A tempest of urges once veiled in darkness
Now conforms from shape and shadow

Color seeps through the walls of existence
The nerves of sentience set in motion
Stories retold through precious stones
An Eden of thought ignites its breath

Brandon Gene Petit

The unwritten quest

One fateful night I follow a voice
Persuaded to leave the comfort I've known
A cry for help from the bowels of oblivion
Comes to me in a subliminal scene

My damsel bound to a distant prison
Her face shadowed by the Devil's claw
A prize beyond the gates of nightmare
Beauty estranged in a spectral swamp

My nemesis guards her in furtive pose
I tap its domain in seek of its face
Weapons minted apart now meet
Again invisible blades will cross

The enemy crouches behind its riddles
Waging the name of my captured love
It reaches out and mirrors my form
Beckoning me to join its world

It reels me in with a cobra's charm
Seducing me into fantasy
Tunneling deep into mental ruin,
I penetrate the empire beneath

Unearthly awe dilutes my fear
No longer a stranger to strangers' lands
An eerie peace will subdue the hero
Who is brave enough to join the prisoner

A journey split into nightly chapters
Installing the parts of an unwritten quest
Through placid days I yearn to end
My hungry heart then guides me in sleep

The call

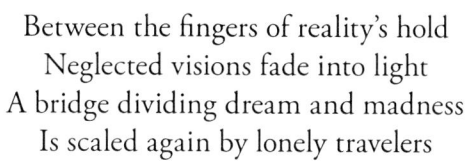

Between the fingers of reality's hold
Neglected visions fade into light
A bridge dividing dream and madness
Is scaled again by lonely travelers

Beyond the fence frontiers await
An addiction to the horizon's end
Fear and courage combined in spell
The bait that triggers a search for self

The angst of elders engraves a trail
Past undivided and nameless lands
Through ambient spheres of insect chorus
A raven to haunt every step of the way

Ancestral cries bellow their names
Calling heirs through the fog of time
Rolling deserts throw painful winds
Eons return with the rising tide

Forest clearings wait for witches
History's bones dissolving beneath
The sparkling cosmos forever turbulent
Mirrored below in a glossy lagoon

Cetacean voices croon their code
Singing their secrets to ocean abyss
Prisms rain on backlit mountains
Restless seasons mold the Earth

These roads are known by wandering minds
Through many months of solitude
They make their home in moving shade
Knitting tales that are never through

Transience

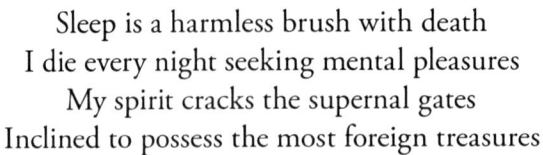

Sleep is a harmless brush with death
I die every night seeking mental pleasures
My spirit cracks the supernal gates
Inclined to possess the most foreign treasures

In waking daze I lurch to my desk
By minimal light I attempt to record
So elusive, that God-given vision
The cryptic message from the night before

I release my pen in mental anguish
Those slippery words cannot be caught
Internal ventures may stem the emotion
Disturbing the depths of world-weary thought

The language of life holds many strange letters
Through song and science these riddles told
The paths of existence unfold eternal
From jungles dark to planets cold

The world a museum of parallel eras
Through darkened glass those visions trapped
A gust of wind from the dawn of time…
Touches my face; the glass is cracked

Back to a blizzard of primal beginnings
Our ancestors bred beneath titanic waves
Sexual chaos sending forth its forms
The ancient code from which progress is paved

Deep in the garden the serpent still dwells
Whispering secrets and tempting with gifts
Forbidden sights lost in his black opal eye
A window to worlds no man can resist

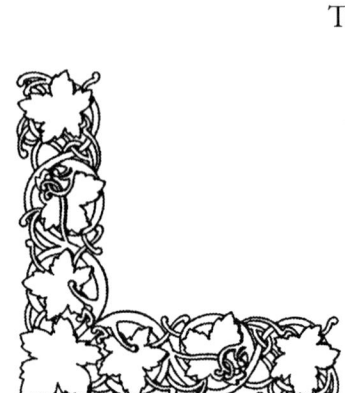

Mysterious objects plucked from dead ages
Adorning the shelves of a curious hall
Infinite stairways of knowledge descending
Only ending upon waking call

Returning to morning with sweat on my brow,
I surface to meet a familiar despair
Those alien vistas now numb to the touch
Concealed in the glow of a cold, blank stare

My gut cries out for receding thrills
Intrepid attempts to revive inner coals
Tasting the fruits of the mind has its price
Eternal debate with my innermost soul

Paroxysm

I lunge after love like a broken winged bird
Pleading for the aid of that calm inner voice
A faceless lover surrenders compassion
I draw her a form to fill a small role

Safe in my mind during mortal turbulence
Her essence confined to a fragile cocoon
Living through bond of pleasure and pain
Together we evade the jaws of apathy

A thorn in my side left from coming of age
Promising reward for surviving trials
Sharing a drink of my sorrow without protest
Absorbing my rage with maternal purpose

Angelic through natural imperfection
Naïve inside of her folded wings
Have I fallen in love with pain?
Or have I realized that pain is love?

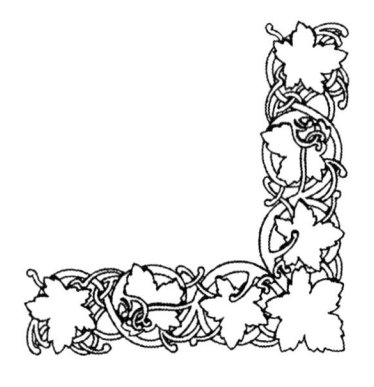

Urban storm

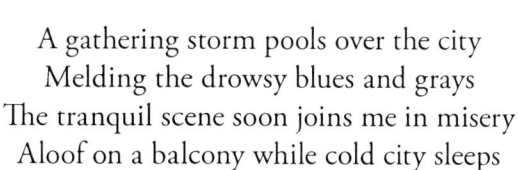

A gathering storm pools over the city
Melding the drowsy blues and grays
The tranquil scene soon joins me in misery
Aloof on a balcony while cold city sleeps

The clouds form an endless shield of gray
Roaming in sync like soldiers to battle
Urges of thunder disturb my trance
Transmitting their deep, subliminal tongues

A chorus of rain then rattles to life
Descending a maze of awnings and gutters
Ribbons of waterfall spill from the roof,
Distorting an image of huddling birds

A church's steeple exposed by lightning
Its drooping bell immune to the wind
Black garden gates aglow with wetness
Aging paint flaking off in the clamor

Streetlights stretched across glistening pavement
Midst an infracted mirror of puddles
Raindrops scratch at draped window clones
Massaging the temples of a world-worn mass

Back in my room the symphony muffled
Thunder runs through a vaulted ceiling
Pale blue light fills a darkened bedroom
As shadows of water stream down the walls

These rainstorms act as mobile seasons
Passing dimensions that alter the mood
Held in trophy these opulent glimpses
For painter and poet a window of rebirth

Scrolls

Tortured minds have written much
The juices of soul wrenched from a cloth
Artists gaze through the eyes of science
A hybrid philosophy is born

Modern grave robbers strive for answers
Thirsting for the jewels of knowledge
Those gazing beyond may never return
Sheltering in those distant corners

The great mortal pain is pursuit of discovery
Curiosity colors our anxious veins
The words left by those now perished
Tempt the next who seek their meanings

The early hours

Dawn unfolds on a town's older region
Sunrise crawls across cobblestone streets
Autumn break speaks its opening words
An urban dream world prepares to awake

I walk these archaic avenues alone
Following the lead of my oversized shadow
Astringent cold awakens my face
While a glinting sun slowly heats my back

Past gothic fencing and cream-colored brick
Concrete bridges veined with vines
Damp shades of wood stare from the park
A fountain shines at the heart of the square

The muffled click of claws against curb
From blackbirds prodding the lower scenery
Shares the air with benevolent fumes
Of bakery bread and chimney smoke

Porch lights fading in soft succession
The radius of light extends its reach
Reflections expanding in dark shop windows
The first opened door soon taints the silence

In time the usual routines exude
An old piece of map slowly stirs to life
Another new chapter from torn, yellowed pages
Is resurrected into tangible shapes

Vestige

A lone man stands a rock against time
Ignorant to the weapons of weather
Sharpening the blade of his internal notions
Using error of past to perfect his future

Bearing a mark, he strays from the herd
His head hung heavy with wisdom and shame
Building a strength out of segregation
Kept by his conscience and trained by regrets

Integrity realized, he grips his defiance
Wrestling for rank in a deity's coils
Pleading for rain from a storm in the heavens
Only love can extinguish his secular fires

Ever in deep with diverse inner struggles
He curses the flood but drinks from the pool
Spending his years under rain and shade
His words his weapon, his thoughts his home

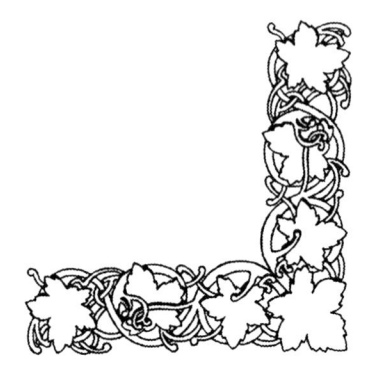

Intrinsic desires

Rivers thick with exotic sentiment
Pour their wine into craving seas
A scavenger along the shores of time
Hunts for displaced memories

A painted sky melts with the ocean's ink
Dusk aflame with dynamic hues
The fiery crimson and lavender light
Exposes a realm of hidden truths

Familiar scents a welcome embrace
Paradise unfolds its arms
Breathing home's assuaging embers
Native to an unearthly charm

Starlight burning prismatic tint
Filling a window with cosmic expanse
Wind chimes echo their turbulent answer
To cosmic winds that distantly dance

Caverns in time attached to the past
By lantern light I search for my brother
Reincarnation extending a quest
Carrying souls from mother to mother

Past and future exchange their roles
Dramatic sequence rearranged
A legacy's leap from peaceful tomb
Immortal while the landscapes change

Memories will walk eternal
Hallowed thoughts in sentient form
Nature shields her favorite spirits
Mother's wing against the storm

Lupus

The predator moves on graceful pistons
Vacillating to instinctual law
Chasing the scents of quixotic terrain
Driven forward by a wild inner sanctity

Conquering distance undaunted by fear
The triumphant rogue content in exile
Stalking the realm of nocturnal vagary
Its spirit preserved in a venerable purgatory

Strengthening from the fuel of its enemies
Seeking to devour the betrayal of brothers
Forever unleashed from temporal binds
Accepting nature as its only god

A universe in solitude

Silence may guard a hundred secrets
The dialect spoken through acts of Earth
Pagan ambitions adrift on a breeze
Travel unchecked through an autumnal realm

A look to the mountains afar in the haze
Injects my heart with strange shades of awe
The still roads purged of moving wheels
Let wind be the only force in motion

Ripples of thought expand with each breath
Dimensions revealed through uncluttered sight
Peace and passion joined at the hip
Inciting adventures beyond terra firma

Whispers of spirits seduce my ears
Retracing their steps back into our age
Sectarian ecstasy ripens my courage
Preparing a departure but not a return

I carry a torch to celestial borders
Enduring a great metaphysical climb
Throwing a light to the darkest fringes
Exposing reality's jeweled inner skeleton

Buried in bliss, I mold my salvation
An outlying blur in society's eyes
Tearing the stratum that stifles my senses
May purity strike me a match in the dark

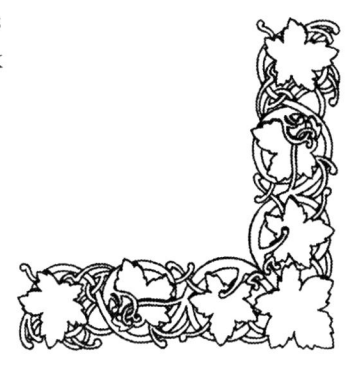

Two

I have walked with both gods and devils
Through the prodigal book of life
Quantum code through erotic visions
Lessons tasted in bittersweet strife

A missing piece completes my soul
A memorable scar once bled my past
I squirm in the fist of a desperate world
Longing to break my solitude's fast

Through darkness I reach for a lover's hand
A companion for the endless walk
Together we seek a lucent Eden
Slipping through time to hear heaven talk

With trembling hands we open the door
Through the archway of ancient marks
We aim to regain the grain of our youth
Far from the evils that tore us apart

The cries of wolves pursue from distance
Into the woodland we're forced to be bold
Pulses pounding, our breath in clouds
Our clutching warmth alleviates cold

Black velvet shadows arrive with nightfall
Curious sounds pan through the trees
A hole in the canopy sparkles with stars
The glimpse of depth brings us to our knees

Frozen with awe we behold the moon
A bond in blood holds lengthy ties
Hand in hand we cross the threshold
Leaving behind all worldly sighs

In morning light we remember our faces
Memories captured of nightly fears
Exit the forest, descending the hillside
A shower of rain pours deity tears

Winding our path through the valley rift
Grazing lips behind waterfall sheets
Heads together on a seaside cliff
Our hearts will never admit defeat

Our voices carry across the plains
Reliving a love that time forgot
Two lost lovers alone in their world
We belong where others do not

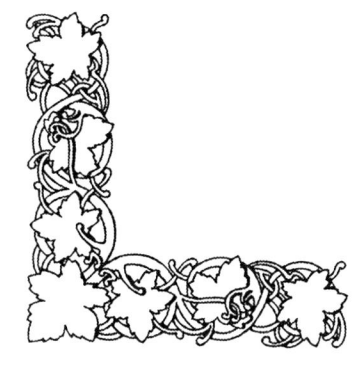

Pathos

A stone standing against the river
A fire writhing beneath a deluge
Drama spreads portentous wings
Avarice makes its bounty huge

Tartarus against the torrent
A pincer set to thunder's call
Good and evil lock their blades
A strife survives till one does fall

Counterparts fulfill their deeds
The stage is set for nature's wrath
Those at war expect no miracles
Moving along the crimson path

Avid players take their places
Helmets closed, all swords are drawn
Beasts of burden give their cries
The curtain raised at burning dawn

Balance broken, scales are tipped
Stories left in tragic wake
What predators became of men
What heroes does a battle make?

Bodies left at fading dusk
Kings and pawns all share their wounds
Heaven's rains make weapons rust
A drink for those that lie in tomb

Temptress

Calling to me with idle lips
The pits of her eyes a beckoning chasm
She proceeds, a serpent in motion
Speaking only by evoking speech

Hypnotist since gift of birth
Preying upon those weak of heart
By pure design a living drug
I'm altered by her necromancy

Mystified by cunning prowess,
I seek a gateway to her soul
Dare of mental chess accepted
The game that guards her fragile core

Mind of woman, will of youth
Sculptured into stunning balance
Poison-riddled antidote
Enriching life at welcome price

Regression

Subdued within these wooden walls
Pacified with a single wish
To live in the past without its true wrath
Backward steps seem more progressive

Reality stalks me, a guiltless predator
Lurking behind every fortunate ending
I pillage its lair in a nervous haste
Determined to stay ahead of its grasp

The world of yesterday still shimmers
A flickering candle refusing to die
Remnants of vistas scattered about
I piece them together like a broken mirror

A huddled timeline of pictures and words
The vivid canal that flows eternal
Angels sketching their deepest visions
I walk through the gallery in a somber daze

At times I return to the vat of anger
Training myself to remembered opponents
When former demons are sweated out
I rest in a cradle of imagined arms

Elusive memories of personal renaissance
Aglow in my mind during stranger hours
The erudite voices that tell of an era
Before my collision with darker forces

Intrinsic Desires

Tenacity throws me against the current
In childish flurries of backwards paddling
Shielding my eyes from tomorrow's light,
I sink in the corner to prolong my stay

The entity known as poetic justice
Will rescue the gifts that I've lost in the end
All pleasures and pains will merge in time
Let patience withstand as the final test

Within and without

From essential strands of primordial weave
Warm life became of that cold, hard clay
Conceived in the womb of inimical void
Before the first light of terrestrial day

Struggling to quell the human machine
An urge to shed new skin overpowers
Mortal endeavors striving for decades….
Having traveled from life's beginning hours

The sting of sapience cries for attention
Experience curls a beckoning finger
Delaying the plague of prosaic decay
Hybrid emotions determined to linger

The eloquent drugs of lies, love and lust
Chemicals bred from ineffable plans
Contorted by nature's loving cruelty
Pristine complected goddess hands

A peaceful flight over planes of existence
The dreams that stir in the minds of the dead
Orphaned monoliths soaking in sunset
Ciphered encryptions remaining unread

Exhaustive throes of euphoric eternity
Impish forms dance in a spherical glass
Oblivion splashed with erratic imagery
The essence that binds all matter and mass

A majestic union of darkness and light
From oil and water to groom and bride
Through the myopia boundaries are breached
The depth and danger along the ride

Spectacle

A gem of lost ages shines blinding light
A spectacle spared for reasons unknown
Left by the gods for the folly of man
Surviving to see undeserving eyes

Revealed at the center of eons unraveled
A trophy polished to honor time's quest
Dripping in ancient aromas long passed
Enticing a flame in all jealous hearts

Fleeting

Leery from your vertigo,
I chased you through the halls of memory
Since then time has blurred your features
Fleeting takes in random show

With seasons passed you shifted form
Now you walk a different plane
I ache to behold your image again
…The innocent shell you left behind

Now you're trapped inside my mind
Banished to some private sector
Color drains from the heart you gave
I struggle to put you back together

With desperate arm I extend my reach
To touch a fragment of your fate
Through corridors of tattered worlds
I seek a path into your life

A wraith that haunts my every routine
Dead to my eyes in a faraway plight
I look for your face in a crowd of strangers
May we meet again in a coming age

Want

Existence bears its common goals
The gain is better than the gift
Outstretched fingertips close bare
The chase prolonged at hope's expense

Swaying to a song of sirens
Noble men soon dock with death
Blind to burdens reality born
Living a lie they won't outlive

Falsely piqued by promised gold
The fool is led to the dragon's den
Fusing greed with valiant schemes
Betrayed by his own leprous acts

Empires crumble to their summit
Columns built on sinking soil
Racing rats pursue their glory
Through a pipe dream ever leaking

Whispers of a soured conscience
Tempted tongue in restless fashion
Standards raised by dancing hands
A throbbing endeavor puppeteered

The taste that draws a flow of tears
Desire plays a cruel device
The sport of mortal men will thrive
Where ambrosia drips from higher ground

For all eternity

The night sky yawns in chilling majesty
Distant fires expel their scents
I stand alone in a moon tinted field,
Inhaling the feverish winter incense

Constellations frozen in warfare
Comets blazing their meaningless paths
I give my respect to this star-smitten chasm
My final home found in the infinite black

Wed to the horizon's ethereal glow
A primeval pull, like moon upon tides
I search for new ways to kindle my spirit
No false light to spoil the place where I hide

My destiny whispered through wind-parted grass
I further my steps, a lone moving pawn
A wilderness stretches before me in elegance
Wading through shadows, a journey is drawn

In many dark hues my figure consumed
Bathing in oneness, I sever all ties
The shape of my fate so easily contoured
Lonesome and bold, a drifter am I

Content in my realm I steer from the dawn
A willing captive of narcotic night
Admiring the black before it turns blue
Just one meager piece of my infinite flight

Clove cemetery

The evening winds converse with the dead
Ignoring the dormant abodes of the living
Bird-less trees reply with a rustle
The language of loneliness fondles their leaves

I wander among the dew-coated headstones
Contemplating each legacy laid
My name not found among the assortment
I'm somewhat dwarfed among the alliance

"Conklin, Edwards, Allen, Schultz …."
The names read off like a tepid parade
The resonance of their distinctive tones
Pounds like a catalyst soon to awaken

The epitaphs scold with a look of importance
Victorian elegance cynically carved
I exit the lot with a trace of naivety,
Leaving the dead to their sober retreat

Alterations

Filters of substance flood me with vim
I rise from the bed where I died last night
Senses align to taste my surroundings
As ancient emotions begin to recur

Through misted mirror a glance is returned
A mentor forgotten extending his wisdom
Coating my simple gray being in gold,
A weapon is made of an ego once lost

Parting the storms that have blackened my faith,
I harness the creature within to contrive
Lifting the dust off a deeper intelligence
Marrying my mind to a greater machine

Ambrosial impulse steers my affections
I follow my will into regions untamed
Sifting through miles of aesthetic clutter
Reclaiming the treasures discarded by fools

Beneath the world's gaze I rebuild my selves
Donning the mask of reclusive indifference
Vulnerable spots now armored in valor
With a poison I enter destiny's jaws

A dying breed

A vampire remembers his dreams in the womb
His skin is as thick as his mind is deep
He wallows in pain but fears not the tomb
Forever in debt to the world that he keeps

He carves out his niche on the eclectic turf
Still true to his form without a complaint
Amorous intentions to prove his true worth
Dodging damnation and stretching restraint

By now he's endured a number of deaths
Each one a release from a subaltern trance
His guile evolving with each newborn breath
Mapping out steps to life's deadly dance

Courage sponges his tears of mourning
Standing in fumes of a well shrouded past
Vengeance narrows his aimless scorning
By dangling finger determined to last

His instincts alone will garner his trust
A man with no master content in his ways
Altered by exile his human form rusts
Making his home in the intricate maze

Molding his figure to troubled times
Risen from dust, his wounds slowly heal
Deeply unhinged by poetic crimes
Exhausted, he searches for life's true feel

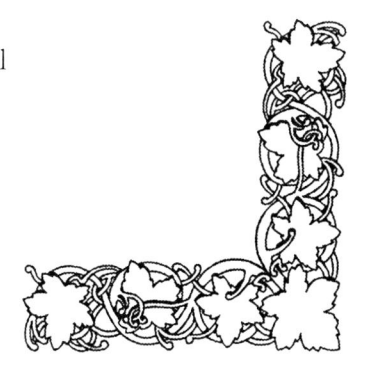

Let me in

When consciousness leaves my toiling mind
I break through the mold of a diurnal prison
My spirit then creeps through a steaming city
To find you lying in a cradle of solace

Drawn to the heat of your sleeping body
A force that caresses your idle face
Watching you dream from an icy window
Entranced by the gentle drum of your pulse

A long, hard road to your soothing embrace
The claw marks of nightmares fresh on my back
Escaping the flesh in the bold midnight air
Yet carnally driven to bask in your aura

Crossing our paths in a lunar lit passage
Meteors flush in the black of our eyes
Emotions entwined like battling serpents
Forever engaged in a beautiful war

Your scent is a guide in the deep subterrane
Perfuming the crypt that I've known for so long
Your breaths softly rock my anger to sleep
Your sweat deeply rinses my spiritual wounds

I leap from a crumbling cliff to your palm
The salt of your being a cure for the venom
Your heart is my body, your body my soul
My warm-blooded wonder in auburn skin tone

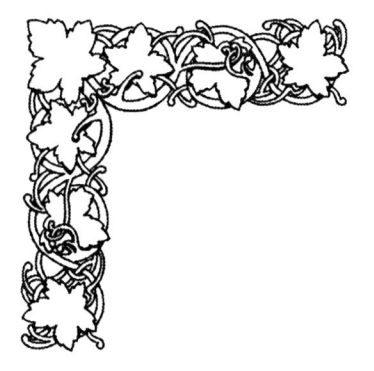

Seeking sanctuary

Battle scars are running deep
Thoughts spill out into disarray
I'm crawling towards eternal sleep
Enchanted comfort kills my dismay

Tired of betrayal's lovable face
Tired of knives that follow my back
How I long for a soothing place
Yearning to walk on a different track

Salvation follows violent grief
The grave a gift compared to war
Sadness rewarding blissful relief
I wonder what death has in store

Under lock and key

Behind closed doors a secret sleeps
Waiting to meet the break of light
Many whispers have spoken its name
Few pairs of eyes have graced its presence

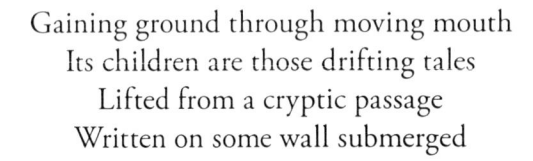

Gaining ground through moving mouth
Its children are those drifting tales
Lifted from a cryptic passage
Written on some wall submerged

Lost to Earth's elusive verges
Separated from their source
Guarded by some livid hound,
Acidic moat or crumbling bridge

A primal breeze completes its rounds
Exhaled from some distant grotto
Carrying with it an elder scent
Torn from the binds of virgin terrain

Wonders crouch from the gaze of day
Striped by the bars of a timely prison
Elder structures safely rest
Where winds of change have been too kind

The roots of modern myth remain
In countless folds of buried progress
Antiquity brought from a lethal age
Stands before fools in a museum case

Some shores are better left untouched
Some stories better left untold
But who are we to break the chain
That links our trivial trials to truth?

Whole

Trust has become a useless organ
Lying limp and dead at your side
A martyr slain in the name of knowledge
To rest in the shadow of your pride

A friend may be a premature enemy
Traitors may wield a thousand masks
Suspicion shines a light within
Catching them at their selfish tasks

Killers' cubs are cute when young
But different breeds divide in time
No more hearts exposed on sleeves
You close the cloak that shows inside

Ignore the pleas that cloud your thoughts
Amend the leak that bleeds your goal
Slash the root that taps your success
Only then can you become whole

Beyond summer

Patience greeted with summer's end
A welcome change unfolding its hand
The incoming fall veneers its craft
An entity ending a cycle of sleep

Cold air leaks in over the hills
As geese give chase to a distant warmth
Leaves awash with a colorful death
Prepare to make their graceful descent

Treetops blasted with puzzling hues
Squarely displayed in a dark-watered pond
The flank of an old barn frosted with vines
The frame of an old car sunken in mud

Pumpkins color a shady churchyard
Varied in size like legions of kin
Coated figures inhabit the street side
Heads held down against the gales

A tarnished statue rooted in stone
Stands in the shade of molting branches
Whirlwinds fraught with nervous leaves
Scurry about its humble slab

An old man sweeps the library steps
A jogger follows a cloud of breath
Children's banter fills an alley
Noon light dims on an empty schoolyard

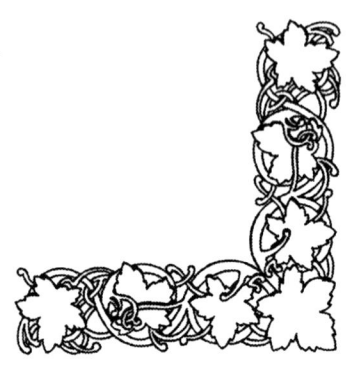

Darkness grows between the trees
Perception marked by lingering fireflies
Purple clouds so gently smeared
Where jet streams scar a tinted sky

Stars begin to reveal their light
As homes reply with glowing windows
People ease their way indoors
Burning the logs that spice the air

Schools and banks now black inside
A full moon paints the sparkling street
Details soft under ebony veil
The canvas cleared for a glimpse of winter

Vomica

A spur embedded within me burns
Vices groan from over my shoulder
I study the hands on the clock as they turn
Mind regresses as body grows older

In time I have made a dungeon of home
Empty eyes glued to a window in vain
Unearth every pain that I've ever known
Each one its own link in a burdening chain

My hands reach out for euphoria's teats
My being shackled for a breach of oath
The starving hound teased by dangling meat
The gift and the curse, I have bred them both

A growing distance keeps me at bay
Driven from joys I had earned in youth
My senses calloused, my hunger restrained
Caught in the web of a thickening truth

Identity spoken through painful words
A jury conformed of abiding foes
The hammer comes down, my fate is ensured
Down to the vault where denial soon grows

Bound with the likes of thieves and liars
Days lurk by as I toy with my past
I lend out my heart to be cast into fire
Strength will become of the bruises that last

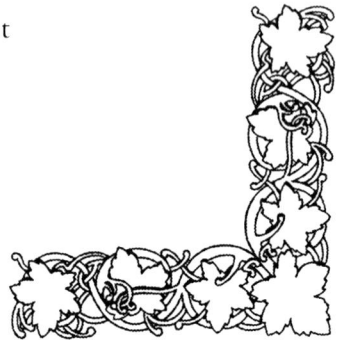

Intrinsic Desires

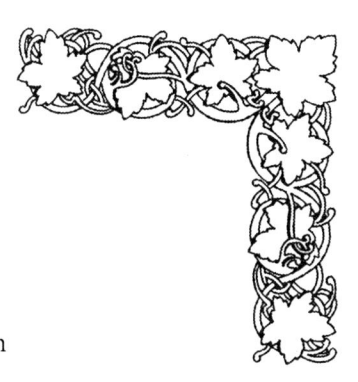

The mark that divides a monster from man
My blood now belongs to a nameless race
Left to the mercy of hourglass sand
My pulse is slowed to reptilian pace

Gorged at the feet of feasting kings
Removing my shell to prove inner power
Fermented pride my suffering will bring
I exit my cell to inherit the hour

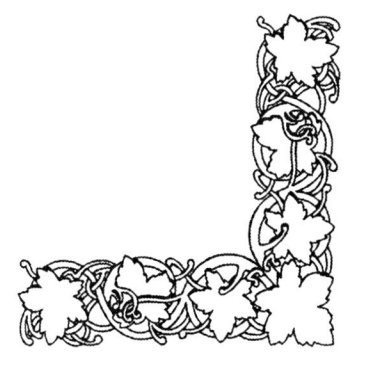

Elsewhere

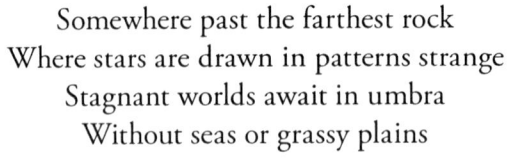

Somewhere past the farthest rock
Where stars are drawn in patterns strange
Stagnant worlds await in umbra
Without seas or grassy plains

Lacking gracious light of moon
Beyond the plumes of raging sun
Stardust shatters into nothing
A battle in which darkness won

Home to blind and nameless phantoms
Strong when earthly fires started
Grazing Gaia's virgin surface
Long before the gases parted

Redolence of cycles ceased
Empyrean compass having fainted
Witness to nocturnal excess
Palettes where no force has painted

Wrinkles on the face of being
Rotted to a gaping hole
Frozen wreckage caught in current
Older than the birth of coal

Lethal, lavish midnight gulf
Poison to the pelt of presence
Blackened tides in twisting spiral
Feed a starving evanescence

Fallen kingdoms never lighted
Victims of the binging void
Answers to our timeless questions
Far from notice are destroyed

Waterfall of things forgotten
Quiet chaos claims its prey
Keys to riddles lost forever
Hells and heavens wash away

Segregated island realms
Home to primal wonders guessed
Roaming out of solar reach
And sailing into unsung deaths

Living eyes will never focus
To this bleak and dead terrain
Fruitless absence ever seething
Out of sight and sound remains

Brandon Gene Petit

Tooth and nail

Ingrained to the days succeeding our idols,
We rattle our dice over dangerous ground
At war with a hindrance our forebears have weakened
The hydra that has but a few heads left

At times the fatigue encumbers our progress
So tempting to lose the chase to another
When life sedates us with anodyne spells
Our thighs may give to the undertow's sway

Mirages play harlot to covetous senses
We drop our nobility to grip self-indulgence
Like termites our vices can hollow our character
Crippling the hunger that brought us so far

But hope's white beam soon pokes through the rubble
A guide to lead us up out of the waste
Again we find our true selves in the light...
Faithfully waiting like glorious steeds

With weaknesses fed and envy contained
We channel our lust to the old straight and narrow
Emotional ties make potent distractions
We brush things like love and charity aside

Leaving old friends to their picture frame prisons
Removing the baggage that anchors our flight
For lengthy travels call for lightened loads
And devoir divides a crowded alliance

People of the fog

I felt as I belonged among those warm yet unfamiliar faces
Mingling of synthetic strangers, one beneath a single roof
Brief nocturnal glimpses given breath inside a stirring mind
How I hate to leave them when the sun finds me awake in bed

Vivid exaltation of some pleasant netherworld event
Friendly beings gathered round, features bright but voices mute
Names were told in muffled whispers, trademark of ephemeral lives
Denizens of transient ties in debt to not a single goal

I drift about their universe of mildly animated twilight
Tourist to a median of ambience well intertwined
Temporary points in space like grains of sand through fingers sifted
Made in mental mists provoked outside the range of naked eye

Dwelling in the narrow cracks where logic cannot intervene
The people of the fog will fade away as fast as they appeared
I feel as though my fate resides with gentle ghosts so self-inspired
Relatives from outer planes that greet me when I douse the light

My ghost walks

A vacant world of my creation
Out of range to reaching worry
Twilight burns a lasting candle
Wheels of time reverse their fury

Dodging carnal coils of envy
Longing I have yet to name
A search for loves I've long since lost
Leads me into sunset flames

My love is now a land so lonely
Ever since I took one breath
This loneliness holds hidden virtues
On a search outlasting death

Empty space reveals no troubles
Only echoes greet my shouts
In silver rain I'm slowly baptized
Sacred drops refine my doubts

Body melts with ocean mist
My footprints swallowed by the tides
Mention of my name will fade
New freedom from the public eye

Journeys without end or aim
Privacy for which I've fought
I peel away these needless layers
Traveling at the speed of thought

Ignis fatuus

*Scottish ruins in London fog
Canadian lakes under African skies
New England clouds on Columbian hills
The great northern lights over rivers in Maine*

An entropic blur of mingled travels
As seen through the eyes of omnipresence
Ladders leaned on the walls of reason
Extremities stretched to infinity's edges

Ambience clipped by a modern world's din
The messages sent from the realm of the spirit
Fairy notes float from arboreal depths
Inspiring the ears of the minstrels who hear it

A hushed summer stashed in an attic of gray
Rain-heavy clouds too many to count
Their bulk looming high over bones in the loch
The riders who've drowned on the wild Kelpie's mount

Castles infracted from dynasties soured
Sentenced to sleep in a vine-woven mesh
Malice is summoned from woodland substratum
A canine design seeking unicorn flesh

Will-o-the-Wisp coaxes drifters at night
At home among oddities nature insisted
Insomnia's trek combs the world's other half
Unfathomed abode of species unlisted

Brandon Gene Petit

From pillars of marble to well guarded gold
Great trials of life on a cavern wall etched
A sundial bathes in a day long forgotten
A day when humanity's limits were stretched

Deities reeking of inhuman likeness
Vented tombs welcoming starlight alone
Legends long buried with curses and jewels
And crystals displayed of peculiar tone

Stories return with the ships that find shore
Sailor minds maddened from journeys so long
Stories submit to the deep salty void
Sailor minds drunken on mermaid's sweet song

Unusual stops on detours of a dreamer
Phenomena shunned by the boldest of maps
Fiction and fact in a blasphemous truce
The globe at a glance and experience on tap

Only human

The flesh I was born into labels my face
A bloodline of bigots, madmen and tyrants
I rescue my name from the media's mouth
By keeping myself out of history's way

A bard introduced into modern day circles
Shedding the notion to trust his own species
I push through the ignorant masses unnoticed
Two cold shoulders guarding me, one on each side

Inventing new flavors of blunt infidelity,
Everyday witchery keeps me unnerved
Dissecting my soul while my mind is astray
To find me with Eve's apple core in my hand

Emotional outlets congested with drama
My own sins enlarged in a tall, twisted mirror
I speak of my ill-fated fiend with a vengeance
…. Only to find his disease at my door

Predictable urges have swallowed me whole
Digesting me down to become a statistic
Too many promises stacked like old bricks
Discolored and cracked from a century's weight

Natural selection mocks my existence
I've grown to become what I hated before
The wisdom I bought wasn't all that I sought
I'm destined to settle for less than I long for

Brandon Gene Petit

Wars between virtue and malice continue
We scatter like ants to dodge their destruction
The traffic of wicked men sneaks by us daily…
Our eyes on the tube like an axe stuck in wood

And so we arrive at the end of my story
The moral assigned now laughs in our face
The best of our leaders may lead us to danger
The bravest of heroes may leave us to rot

Parted ways

A well hidden bruise where our lives intersected
A heartache I stopped only briefly to ponder
Immune to the pull of such magnetic grief
Where you melted in the arms of uncanny persuasion

My fears became real when our bondage grew soft
Your will power failed my faith in humanity
Against that closed door I listened in horror
Your need for my love had been purchased by evil

Escape opened up but your head was distracted
I chose to tread water, you fell limp and drowned
You just couldn't leave when the world called for me
I finally turned to my own selfish ties

Taming retentions whose fangs have been waning
Oblivious to mental exhibits retired
No more ropes tossed to a childhood flame lost
I tend to the one who's been waiting inside me

De novo

There I was beneath gray skies
Knee-deep in the moans and sighs
After fall of man; alone
Heir to a dead city's throne

Lost between unfinished walls
Guideless in the empty halls
Towers down to nothing shook
Broken toys and burning books

Once again the statue weeps
For the grudges ghosts will keep
Finally, things went too far
All the way to ash and tar

Not a sound to wake the dead
Crooked in their scattered beds
Smoking plains of wonders cruel
Closure for a nuclear duel

Forms bereft of living schism
Sum of stringent cataclysm
On my morbid wonder leads
Over rows of drowning seeds

Vandalized by bitter cold
Left to hang in silent hold
Great accomplishments of man…
Crushed like castles in the sand

Intrinsic Desires

Rain released for pity's sake
Clutter left for *Them* to rake
Ones who've traveled solar miles
To reclaim the fertile piles

Terraform the barren clay
New arrivals have their way
Healing all that fire singed
A genesis impels again

Idle hands

I won't fall prey to the old cliché
No last requests for a second chance
So easily marred is this mortal clay
Defeated in its brief romance

I'll carry no blame in this foolish game
Erase my name from the audition list
I find a place among many a face
A spectator cloaked in ignorant bliss

I linger behind these passive eyes
A ghostly scout in a window upstairs
Looking away to autarkic skies
Over the heads of the unaware

There lies a hole where I'm to be sold
The system breaks where I've cheated fate
I'd much rather cling to a personal mold
Than slaughter my angst and participate

I'll extend not a limb past the spotlight's edge
I'll leave not a dent on this cluttered map
Since years of youth I've honored the pledge…
Never to snare my foot in the trap

Life is a liquid that ripples when touched
Fortune and fame may inspire decay
Shape is corrupted from changing too much
I step out of line and engrave my own way

Things to come

Behold the new horizon as it shines upon a rose revealed
Rays of mellow light descend from cool blue evening clouds again
Killing fields have been remodeled into uneventful dream
The fiery gates of hell have long since smothered under tangled vines

Horror's wilted features now withdrawn into a hooded darkness
Consequence of ill reform recedes with newly broken spell
Demon shoulders bound with yokes, malicious armies spreading thin
Let them fall to nether reaches miles below our line of sight

Standing on the welcome mat of infantile Elysium,
A weary beggar reunited with a wealth of simple pleasures
No more feeling blindly through a coma's psychotropic lair
Squinting at the daylight after years behind a pointless gloom

Parasitic recollections doomed to feed a passing chaos
Fears are seized and scrambled to begin a cleansing of the mind
Heightened senses conquer famine, hypnotized by beauty's breath
Harmless shards of muzzled rage now hung like pictures in a home

Limbs of progress growing quickly, equilibrium restored
Loose ends tied in sacred knots to end the nauseous apparition
Qualms expose their hidden angles, answers found that weren't before
A practice most comparable to feeling multi-sided gems

Branching off to lesser roads that lead back to simplicity
Apart from scores of counted heads that still pursue a villain's glory
Freedom falls on endless pastures, lurking threat of vultures gone
A sturdy mesa built upon the fossils of our former selves

Still there

When your only mission becomes submission
When promise leads to a compromise
I'll still be there at the fork in the road
With empty pockets and arms open wide

When gold has withered to dust in your hand
And roses meant for your lover have dried
I'll still be there at the fork in the road
With empty pockets and arms open wide

When faith refuses to come out of hiding
And people you trust have admitted they've lied
I'll still be there at the fork in the road
With empty pockets and arms open wide

When worlds you've known have been painted over
And copasetic has lost its prime
I'll still be there at the fork in the road
With empty pockets and arms open wide

When leaders have melted back into the masses
And family's packed up and left you behind
I'll still be there at the fork in the road
With empty pockets and arms open wide

When trials of age have bleached your beauty
And all you have left is your sorrow and pride
I'll still be there at the fork in the road
With empty pockets and arms open wide

Disenchanted

Misery seeks my hand in friendship
Bitterness waits for my likely fall
Jeopardizing my humble creed,
The future patiently chooses a shape

How will I finish this test of sanity
Still retaining the same old face?
No use retracing old intentions
Knowledge flaunts its cynical frown

The wool that darkened my eyes is gone
But now they are met with atrocity's sting
Must every pure white sheep façade…
Mask a lupine foe in wait?

Structure cannot be sustained
With so many vital pieces missing
Mind games weave a maze around me
Each new dawn conveys new riddles

I look back at my beaten path
Where two of many questions stalk me
How have I managed to come this far?
And how much more will I endure?

Head held high over clouded waters
As tremors of change reach deep within
Regrets are left to the wind in ashes
A season of tears now ends in drought

Withdrawn

You won't see me show my face
Until the sun dies in the west
A flaming funeral to my left
A subtle sinking in my chest

I then step out to smell the air
Appearing from a murky door
Where I had stood some nights before
To wish away my daily sores

I muse before a cooling yard
Then wipe me off a dusty chair
Reclining into evening care
So sated, calm, and self-aware

A simple-minded book in hand
With which I half pretend to read
A chance for ailing mind to feed
To satisfy a harmless need

Suggestions of untold events
Soon come to me in failing light
Somewhere between the wrong and right
In privacy of hindered sight

The echoes of a barking dog
Blue lights atop a distant tower
Atmosphere of later hours
Comes to aid with healing powers

Breathing night with porch-light off
Is something I should do more often
Makes my rigid posture soften
Keeps away an early coffin

Maybe I should call somebody
Wait, I'd rather be alone
My tired hand hangs up the phone
Content and stubborn as a stone

Theophobia

Sadness is an island that I visit when my life permits
Indulging in parole before your minions see that I have gone
Hurried steps on waning pavement bring me down to water's edge….
There I take a shoddy boat and set out for a place to mourn

Even on that phantom rock where waves lash out to touch my feet
I feel your eyes awaken like an itch demanding cool remission
Beaming down obsessively, igniting flames upon my neck
Followed by a brutish voice that mocks me in my fetal state

Judgment crashes through the ceiling, crippling what I thought was sky
Once again unwelcome phrases filter in to weigh me down
Scorn has rediscovered me, a satellite that never dies
Pity from the outside growing thinner with each secret sold

Where can this well rattled soul escape your ever burning gaze…
And find a place too deep or high to lose my poltergeist behind?
You dry my tears without consent, then stand me on my feet to fall
I curse your quiet laughter when my back is turned to tilted ears

Where can these frustrated fists unfold to make two praying hands
When a small black cloud pursues me even through a great cathedral's hall?
Ones that cupped their hands around my innocence now predisposed
Dirt that I had kicked in spite now lies beneath my bended knee

I watch your figure rise behind me as I kneel to splash my face
Your statuesque expression pours disgust around my shattered will
A ceremony follows to divide me from your kingdom kin
You play the circling buzzard while I play the tortoise on its back

Plenty of time

"There's plenty of time for love," she'd say
The words hung harsh in my head that day
So much depends on a teetering plot
Of whether I trust in our fate or not

A tentative ear holds back her hair
So strange how she doesn't seem to care
Her patience can make me doubt our love
So fresh and aloof, a silent dove

She shies away from the outstretched hand
Still turning her back to devotion's command
Her dreams soon came to take her away
With hidden regret, I had chosen to stay

Kicking her heel, so perfect and proud
The poise of her voice now a weakening sound
The image of her at her usual art
Will fade with security found at the start

At times it hurts but I just cannot blame
This sturdy young woman so caught in her fame
An orchid encountered in habitats mild
Retaining integrity, left in the wild

Touch is no option, telepathy frayed
Our heads in the clouds, facing opposite ways
Its weird how our lives interact then let go
We see the same moon but we won't ever know

The art of forgetting

Rolling on New England hills
A drowsy passenger en route
Settling into torpid cadence
Eyes at rest on distant targets

Rescued by reluctant angels
Just before the final blow
A relict of a sinking vision
Novice to a rural spell

A reign of hurt made obsolete
Old fires ebbed by filthy snow
The piercing glare of winter white
Compels blue weary eyes to squint

Dipped in semi-sweet surrender,
Puppet strings fall limp at last
A bale of wants and woes now rests
In the belly of a day deceased

Birds in flight, a living symbol
Cruising through antique asylum
Hopes to one day join their freedom
Race against the blur they ride

Home assumes initial form
Condemn the roads that led astray
The land of all things left behind
Becomes a brand new destination

The fifth column

They joined their hands in secrecy
And bargained over candles black
Exceeding all their usual schemes
To hone a new breed of attack

The pooling of assorted powers
Perfect enemies at large
Their wicked worlds align with mine
A cruel elite prepared to charge

One to use my past against me
Carrying out a bloodless crime
Keeper of the document
That lists the downfalls of my time

One to steal a former love
And lead her into deadly shade
Mocking my corroding heartstrings
Watching my resilience fade

One to lure me in with lust
Then spear my heart when I grow soft
Draining 'til the thrill has left me
To her only self betrothed

One to drown my name in slander
Handing me the dirty blade
Covering up his fleeing tracks
And leaving me with debts unpaid

Brandon Gene Petit

One to tempt my swallowed anger
Offering me a chance to steer
Dealing out impassive wisdom
In exchange for loyal fear

This antagonistic tribe
Is made of all who dare conspire
Each one with a drive to feed
Will plague me 'til my days expire

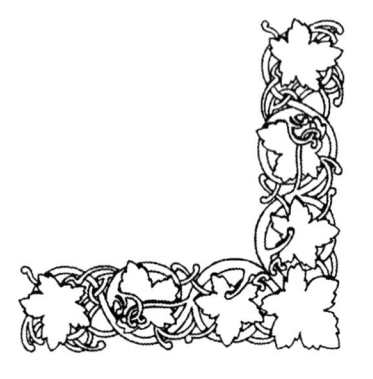

Gray

Naked trees wet with a winter declined
Reach out to claw at the storms that consolidate
Avian chatter returns to the block
In the arms of a gnarled oak polished by mist

Spring smuggled in by ingenious disguise
A peasant-dressed czar in drenched, dismal garb
A timid newcomer delaying transition
Still crouching backstage before the inception

The faint drips and cracks of a moistening Earth
Give life to an anti-industrial realm
A mockingbird's dissonance breaks from above
His blasphemous melodies sculpting white noise

The gaping abyss of an afternoon fog
Swallows the far end of little known roads
Rarely disrupted by glaring white headlights
Hiding the driveways to little known homes

Bloated clouds straining to hold in their bounty
Ooze their way eastward to reach distant shores
There they will paint their immaculate sheets
Where fragments of prism stain through the haze

A stiff lake embodies an ocean of gray
It's flawlessness spared by the absence of breeze
A damp empty love swing hangs unexploited
An ode to a time for absence and zen

Brandon Gene Petit

A million still beads of water at rest
Impeccably formed on a clean wooden glaze
Small squares of dew suspended in place
Reside in the grid of a tattered screen door

The hands on the clock seem to linger much longer
When pushing through air of a thick saturation
Haunted by things of a less modern nature….
The strong supernatural pull of the past

The same frozen sky that rests on the fields
Will shiver the spine of a sailor at sea
Rocking the sign of a store on the boardwalk
Provoking the wary to wind up their anchors

A loitering sense of sublime renovation
Stretches from cobblestone corner to coast
Superbly enacting the Passover's power
With night will erupt an unsilenced release

In stride with giants

Buildings bathed in blinding sun, great silver stalks that hurt to glimpse
A place for men to thumb through money; bees and honey…. dollars, cents
Stairways leading up to find the ballroom floors and penthouse suites
Home to both the self-made man and those who ride on others' feats

Thralls that trade their names for numbers, camouflaged by barcode stripes
Voices held in flawless chorus, each one tuned to different pipes
Those who lag behind are crushed and gathered by a passing broom
No one dares to cool their pulse; a leering clock in every room

Royal cups will overflow while peasants work behind the set
Blistering their filthy hands while floors above ice sculptures sweat
Some retreat to greener prospects, shedding their neurotic skin
Those who make it find some lake to drown their city sorrows in

Separating gold from sand, a witch-hunt style eugenic reign
No remorse for common folk; the best of blood resists the drain
Helpless in a concrete crypt, they reach in vain to touch the blue
Out where soaring hawks befriend the pollen winds and lost balloons

History will never sway; the present just a new disguise
Pyramids still built on slaves except they now wear suits and ties
Crowds of men with painted cards connect to form one massive face
Children in a land of giants; buildings, mountains, outer space

Doors and hallways

I spend all my time in this dismal world
Trying to find a sane way out of it
Choices and queries make unlabeled paths
Conveyors that lead to demises in question

This world can make enemies out of strong lovers
Reduce great craftsmen to helpless dreamers
I scramble to find my place in the chaos
But soon my niche is invaded by others

A step to the right leaves me well overcrowded
A step to the left leaves me lost and alone
Trying to please everyone in my way
Without doing harm to my inner complexion

Separate identities tug at my temper
From rebels enraged to soothsayers sage
A line of descendants projected behind me
Awaiting their turn at the helm of my brain

A nomad unsure of his next destination,
I foster a purpose in all of my efforts
Determined to make the entire trip blindfolded
Deaf to the warnings of prophets back home

Teaching myself not to sink in my sorrows,
I suck all the juice out of every mixed blessing
Eager to nurture my unapproved courage,
I cling to my karma through gutter and grace

Intrinsic Desires

I pass through the legs of a colorblind god
My dreams too complex for that kind of heaven
I carry my sins across neutral terrain
Each hill, a new test, lights a fire in my chest

Caught in a whirl of unrecognized crossings
Dizzying halls of a puzzled pursuit
Each doorknob warm with the life force inside
I leap from dead space to a new point in time

The peaks and the troughs experienced the same
My apathy turns to a new guessing game
More doors await every turn, every bend
The kind that will lead to more hazardous trends

Misanthrope

My smile is only temporary, remnants of a broken face
It sees right through the walls of people, traveling at a sullen pace
I hold the door for elder folk, I laugh at children's silly jokes
Only to resume my role as an ogre whose interior is cold

Lost in periodicals or staring at my twitching feet
They wish to travel elsewhere, for I'm restless in your company
Must be going, can't be late, an unknown place of interest waits
Evening done, a meal for one, my bedfellow the setting sun

A painting of the savior's face; his frozen features look away
Is he mad or is he sad ? I still can never tell to say
Maybe he's ignoring me; he'll wait no more for my repentance
If I met him on the sidewalk, would he say a single sentence?

Cut off at the shoulders, there's no room for open, loving arms
I pass the picture everyday, dismissing its confusing charm
Mona Lisa's male equivalent, taut expression twisting truth
A giant on exhibit, ever distant and so much aloof

I'll get by with one more sigh, for pride is just a one man sport
Reverb gives a brief reply, a lonely surround-sound retort
Prudent forces from outside will never eat their way to me
No more shepherds made to follow, telling me what I'm to be

Everywhere I look I see my life spread out across the walls
Avoiding all the record keepers, hoping I'll forget it all
A part of me is worth the rest of everything that I adore
I am everything I need; I'll call upon you nevermore

Her

The back of my mind is a strange place indeed
A wilderness crammed with diverse apparitions
A messenger comes to me out of the bedlam
And offers a vision that hints of her face

In delicate moments I follow her progress
Her cycles of sadness and fits of contention
I witness her birth from a gathering of light
A multitude of disheveled aromas

She entered my life in a time of despair
Just when I thought of unlocking my death
She served as a crutch for a thrice broken heart
I traded my ire for a new kind of hurt

Now I'm behind the glass where she dwells
Dimming the places I once roamed alone
A beast to her beauty, I drank from her hand
Cut by the thorns of a mishandled rose

Her laughter can summon a mist to my eye
Her genuine innocence truly unreal
She gathers my ashes, my honor replenished
Purpose returns to the flow in my veins

Beyond the days where time had no meaning,
Beyond denial I dared to wonder…
Is she a permanent portal to glory?
Or an ephemeral brush with elation?

Brandon Gene Petit

Our happiest days were backlit by tragedy
I knew that, someday, I must let her go
The pearly white hand that pulled me to safety
Did not deserve to be crushed in my grasp

Besides, true love is not that important
As over-rated as candy and wine
Wisdom is greater than women and wishes
I'm much better off staying close to my kind

The touch of Eros

A substance stirs behind the curtain
Tied into the mortal chest
Inscribed among the cogs and cobwebs
Found within the purest flesh

An old world healer gone askew,
He makes unlikely eyes attract
No pity for the arrow-struck
The makings of a jealous pact

He offers every pleasing form
And puts it up for friendly trade
Then drags you through a drunken dance
A milestone in his promenade

He tampers with your mental wires
And finds a way to silence guilt
Designed to take your breath away
And make your innate morals wilt

Just moments after being bitten
Mindful logic redefined
His victims sleep in godlike hold
Priorities get left behind

He waves a wand before your eyes
And misdirects you with a glare
Intending to derail your judgment
Stripping till your will is bare

Brandon Gene Petit

Selfish lust consumes you whole
Surrounds you with a solemn feast
For once you sit it seals you in
A prisoner, to say the least

Eros laughs, the trap is full
His sideshow wins a brand new tool
The warnings given die unheard
When Eros leads the waxing fool

Look down

You jumped the gun and threw the first stone
Then cowered behind the leg of your god
I've done my time, survived the lashes
Clubs and torches have vexed my door

Just look down as I enter the room
Exclude me from your peripheral vision
My conscience works, I can punish myself
I don't need you to awaken my shame

You had to pour salt on my open wounds
But don't lose footing while kicking me down
For my disease can be spread with ease
One day you'll inherit this thorny crown

Diem ex die

At home, within range of all comfortable sounds
So far from the outside abyss I am found
In lantern-lined shadows, surrounded by books
The inner world calls with a sweet baited hook

Adventure unearths, here comes my new ship
An imagined device for a generous trip
A daydreaming hermit will dutifully thrive
In cosseted pockets of leisurely time

A personal flight I've been meaning to catch
The starlight to guide me, no console or deck
I'll fly to the sun without getting a burn
I'll fly to the moon, but tonight I'll return

I'll fly to a palace on red desert dunes
Past Indian valleys and Druidic runes
I'll fly to a place that was once out of reach
A Venusian sky or Devonian beach

I'll slice through auroras of colors divine
And creep through a crack in the fabric of time
I'll tame all the beasts with a mystic command
And wow all the kings with a trick of my hands

I'll soar through the seas on a winged manta ray
And witness Atlantis in stunning decay
I'll pilfer lost gold from a reef-studded wrack
And on the return seek a pirate attack

Intrinsic Desires

I'll climb to a terrace unwritten by man
Whose last tenants were a pre-hominid clan
I'll map out a jungle and outlive a curse
To earn a return, I am surely the first

I'll sing with the gypsies and pray with the monks
I'll play with the lock on some illicit trunk
I'll conquer the world that my mind let me borrow
And ride on the tails of impending tomorrows

I have no objection to living such lies
These jaunts open up just to answer my sighs
I tap into thought with the greatest precision
Reverie seeps in through a tiny incision

The series progresses and so do my skills
My methods in fighting the boredom that kills
A bard that makes up for the things that he lacks
I wish that one day I will never come back

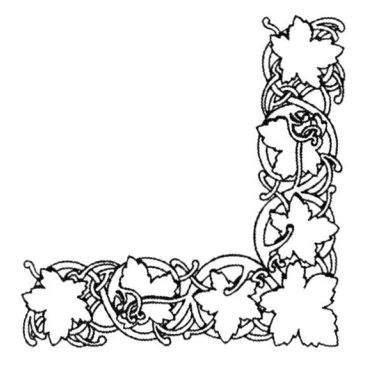

The intercession

Let the night air singe my lungs
And greet me from the eastern fields…
Through which her steps will shortly cross
To meet me in this formal hour

Followed by a wily crew
Of those who've come to seek redemption
Refugees from dying days
Protectors of a life disdained

Her features damp in silhouette,
She lights a lantern scarce of fuel
Then opens up that yellowed book….
Its pages twitching in the wind

A silent joy is well redeemed
We hurry for the morning nears
Brave companions clasp their hands
United through a furtive chant

Winter voices hoarse and hollow
Rise and fall in quaint accord
Words derived from ancient text
Live again in frosted form

Break of light sends us astray
Dispersed just like a flock of crows
Out of character we shrink
Until it's time to meet again……

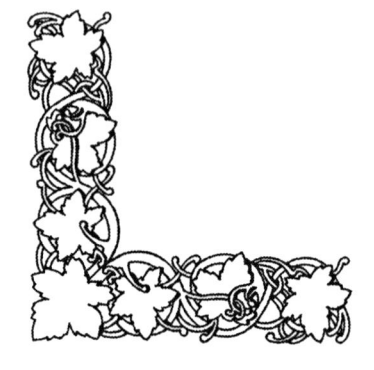

Epitomes

The hand that used to steal in hunger
Eats with silver spoon alone
Hands that wield a sword for good
May plot to steal the Devil's throne

The hand that feeds a biting mouth
Will lose an arm to futile pity
Hands that build a private life
Bleed less than hands that serve a city

Canines raised by heartless master
Greet the world by showing teeth
The soured youth of broken home
Rebuilds himself in seedy streets

Men that keep in step with wolves
Will never tend to beggars' pleas
For those that work and fight to live
Will never waste time on their knees

Eyes that saw the fall of Rome
Will never see a man in space
Minds that dreamed a flattened Earth
Had never dreamed an alien race

The mouth that spreads the whitest lies
Will face the truth before the end
The ears that lead to boring minds
Will always welcome truths that bend

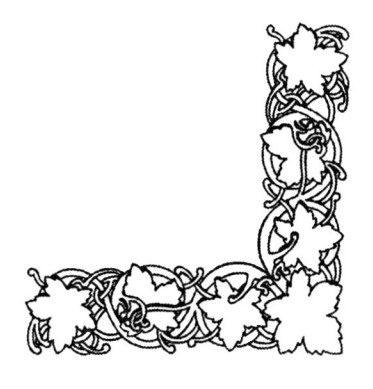

Deeper still

Gone are the days of dragons and knights
Those episodes shrunk down to murals and busts
A new epoch stirs at the edge of perception
Hiding some "dragons" of its own

You might stop at those common tales
Those images fit your juvenile fancy
My mind lusts for a truth unadorned
A truth that surpasses the foibles of fiction

I am a curator of intangible things
I dare to chip the enamel that guards…
A place that has always escaped our detection
A world that unfurls upon God's hidden hand

I walk through the gardens of unguarded madness
Tending to brush against oddities spawned…
In the worlds that babble to me in my sleep
And slither between my legs unnoticed

A fever to quench of peculiar caliber
Drives me to reach for the loftiest chimeras
A black portal throbs and whispers my name
Where foreign light lingers upon the inimitable

Outlandish scents leak through with the vapors
Born in that musty old labyrinth of wonder
An elder charisma rewards the transition
My mortal sobriety slips through my hands

Intrinsic Desires

Demons and specters won't turn me away
Bewilderment nails me to where I now stand
Call me a madman, I'll answer with silence
I came here to see what there is to behold

So leave you your dragons, griffins and unicorns
Here, magic goes by a different name
My eyes caught a spark in the dark of a doorway
Don't try to follow, you won't understand

Evening eyes

Trembling tip of candle flame, reflecting in the windowpane
Does its hypnotizing dance inside a dark, cerulean frame
Staring through it grips me so, in darkness of the dining room
The evening prematurely dim; so sleek in its seducing gloom

Center of this empty house, a fireplace that chirps and cracks
Deep inside my humble shrine of burning wood and bleeding wax
Silence plays a violin to hypnotize my mental foes
Winds outside will soon join in and calcify my cares and woes

A sleeping cat, an empty plate, before me in this hour of late
My consciousness has done its deed, now slowly starts to dissipate
My eyes will soon play tricks on me, new phantoms in the darkness form
Fuzzy black amoebic shapes contorting here within the dorm

The time has come to draw the shades and put away the world outside
Midnight has a bed that's made, prepared to rest my meeker side
Now it's time to put to rest my nervous fears of destiny
I close my eyes and visualize as though my home were by the sea

Bring you to life

There you lay flat on a thin, glossy page
A runway on screen, or a spotlight on stage
From cheekbone to collarbone golden and glistening
Beauty assured at the time of your christening

Emerald green eyes, or as blue as the skies
The distance between us so greatly outsized
Your aura and style are as sharp as a knife
Oh lord, how I wish I could bring you to life

Circa 1988

I still remember that daylight realm
A renaissance rooted in rich juvenilia
Before the brisk tides of advancing change
Began to close in on my childhood predictions

My thoughts still turn to those static porches,
Dull green lawns and somnolent streets
Where seasoned houses armored in brick
Stand firm in a drowsy, humid haze

Where concrete sparkles in sweltering sunlight
And parked cars shimmer with judicious colors
A warm breeze gradually infects each block
Equipped with the tang of freshly cut grass

Sundry scents from sun-faded flowers
Radiate from a vine-crippled fence
Blue jays sip from a half empty birdbath
Oak trees spill over dappled curbs

Backyard clutter and neglected toys
Wait idly by between the houses
Staring from behind a chain-length gate
With the slightest trace of human sadness

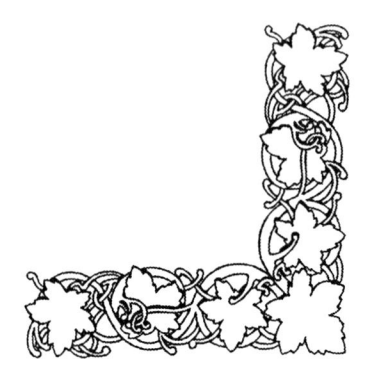

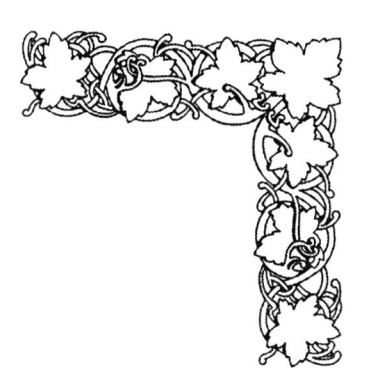

The temperate drone of evening cicadas
Rises and falls like a mock ocean shore
A lawn sprinkler chatters, an evident metronome
Soaking a sidewalk in effortless strokes

Suburban sorority gathers its nest
As pulses decline in unsung isolation
A peaceful oasis of untainted sanity
Waits at the end of all journeys deterred

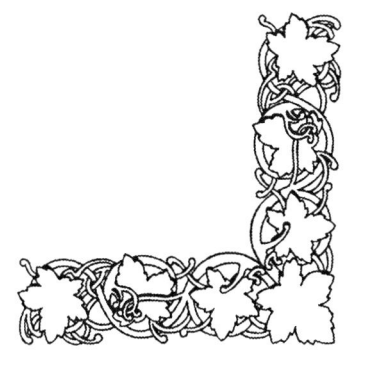

Cruentus

I stand in sheer amazement at the monster that I can't recall
The war machine that runs on fractured egos and rejected wishes
One last rush will pull me off a finger slick with perspiration
Swore I'd never fit that role, but evolution drags me on

The planet seems to throb with my exerted breath and desperate sighs
As pressure builds from swatting at the disembodied criticism
Euthanizing future guilt, refusing offers of escape
An orchestra of soulless hiss compels me to promote my presence

Driven mad by crimson tones I flung myself at sickly odds
A power trip descending from a cobweb tucked away within
Although the drama made me stronger than my idols ever did,
I'd trade it all for open air, cold fluids and a woman's touch

Throwing burdens overboard, rewarded with their priceless shock
The product of a narcissist experiment now under way
A final leap connects me to the saga of dishonest circles
Safety found on neutral ground discarded like an infant's toy

Fever dreams

Ghastly figures chiseled from a seething, anomalous darkness
Fill my morbid fantasy with winged and leathered hides of gray
Holding in their moistly gleaming claws a glass of wine or grapes
Gathered in a ghoulish ball festooned with banners black and red

A band of most unsightly minstrels guides the anesthetic stupor
Sawing at their stringed devices; cellos voiced in guttural groans
A cast of creatures great and small obeys the sweltering sonata
Leaping, spinning, laughing forms not left without a touch of grace

Fountains belch a smoky furor, boiling their contrasting colors
Decked like replicated swamps complete with lily pads and weeds
All alive with insect song convening with the strings and cymbals
Flaunting scores of fish-like creatures beautiful but dire to touch

Priceless fixtures, busts and vases; tribute to inhuman craft
Sharing light with weird and wondrous jewelry rattling in the mist
Gargoyles send their glances downward, backed by paintings smeared with lore
Colossal tapestries that tell of battles, feasts, and hybrid beasts

Outside an oddly tinted sky beams down, a condescending god
To light a horrid greenhouse crammed with nameless fruits and feral plants
Each one armed with tempting tastes to seal the fates of careless grazers
Tangible companions to the notes of steely, twisted passion

Lights begin to dim upon this whimsical yet fierce charade
As stranger sights emerge from hiding, well equipped to tease the eye
A tousled bird residing in a wooden cage calls out the hour
Black as the advancing night that soon replaces skylight glare

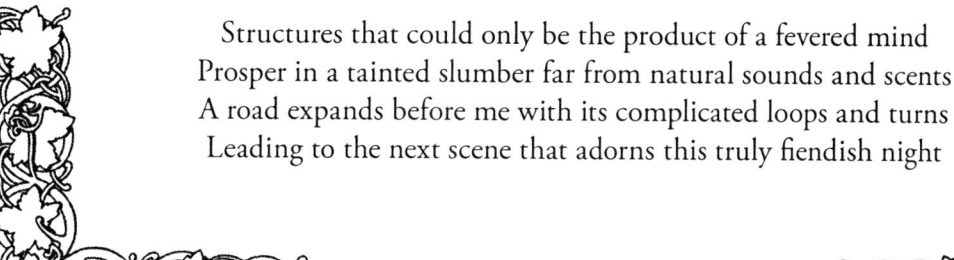

Structures that could only be the product of a fevered mind
Prosper in a tainted slumber far from natural sounds and scents
A road expands before me with its complicated loops and turns
Leading to the next scene that adorns this truly fiendish night

Matris

It's hard to believe that you were one
Within yourself before my time
An era that I'll never see
When you were young and I was nil

I wrap you up in paranoia
Now your fears have come full circle
No one dares to hurt you here
Behind the bars of my ardour

My greatest fear is that you'd take
A bullet that was meant for me
I avow to put you first
And put you safely out of reach

When you're gone, the world will end
In fire and ice and angry winds
All blown away, for all I care
I'll curse the dawn if you're not there

Words alone

Words alone cannot describe
This nameless feeling that I hide
It finds me when I hear something…
That strikes a chord and lets it ring

De ja' vu with expectation
Happiness in moderation
Ecstasy with fear of losing…
True blind faith while vainly musing

Subtle waves of incoherence
Purity plus interference
Apprehension disengage
Useless once it goes away

Anticlimax waits ahead
In clouds I strive to keep my head
Exaltation will depart
Victory leads back to start

Listen

My eyes grow wide to hidden forces
Hair restless in the breeze
A pleasant wind that stops and starts
Its pauses filled by spiritual pleas

Over time I've learned to listen
To the creak of inner gears
Growing stronger, reaching farther
Gazing through my thinning fears

Children's laughter echoes falsely
Haunting in the barren street
Dimmed by ponderings of existence
Irony beneath their feet

The traffic of my mixed emotions
Rises over shingled roofs
Standing on a giant's shoulders
Reaching for a higher proof

The mission is to redesign
The world that I have known so well
A sacrifice to reenlighten
Frees me from an unseen hell

Questions without consequence
My faith is a forgotten art
Alienation makes me wise
From childish things I must depart

The lever is unholy sight
That pierces through the vanity
A third eye slowly blinks to life
I'm knowledged beyond sanity

Long before you cease to live
I see the ghost that bides in you
Widening senses ever swift
My shots are blind but my mark is true

The sensorium

Trapped between two mirrors in a world behind reality
Where the air is a drug and time is merely futile sarcasm
Both life and death have disappeared into one communal grave
Leaving me stranded in a temple of night-colored daydreams

Back doors lead to a potent dawn, vibrant with incessant glory
Holding in its grasp colors from some perversely alien rainbow
A blazing spectacle not unlike that of a dying phoenix,
Reflecting off the opaque crystals that were once my sightless eyes

An endless spiral staircase twists, a ribbon of amethyst velvet
Through an oceanic void bejeweled with candle-spotted darkness
Falling apart step by step where windows coincide with doors
And the dreams of children flirt with the musings of the mad

She lies across the back of my mind in a turbulent sleep
Striped by the silhouettes of steel bars and open window blinds
Her skin made of diamonds, scales, and unfamiliar voices
Her hair revolving scents to match the seasons in my veins

I lick the inner flavors from her warm, watery eyes
Absorb it and turn myself a thousand shades of faded green
Lost inside a tumbling tide of foreign coins and falling objects
Much like being trapped among the intricacies of a Persian rug

I refuse to awaken, to decide on a form or a feeling
Instead I prick my finger with the needle that she made
And at once suffer a wealth of the wildest emotions
Sensations that surround me like a curling wisp of fragrant smoke

Intrinsic Desires

The clock ticks eons past twelve, drifting into strange new numbers
Symbols that tell a distant future the present grips in secrecy
I'm a scar on this virgin skin of existence, a crack on a broken watch face
Through pulsing metallic gills I breathe the synthetic serenity

A tingling sense of childlike awe prolongs my paradox obsession
Dizzy with forbidden questions, I drop down yet another rung
I belong here as a god but can change or affect nothing
As my soul turns to liquid and slips through my quivering hands

Noctivagus

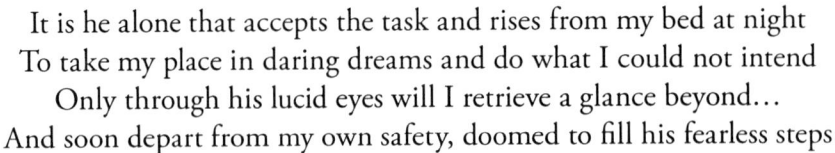

It is he alone that accepts the task and rises from my bed at night
To take my place in daring dreams and do what I could not intend
Only through his lucid eyes will I retrieve a glance beyond…
And soon depart from my own safety, doomed to fill his fearless steps

Down to twisting caverns lit by geode gardens strangely bright
Through spider web complexity and doubtful depths of dragon sleep
Where fumes of steaming lava spring invade a grotto's dusty lungs
And skulls of long forgotten creatures break down into transient powders

Oily black abandoned vaults that never know the changing months
Strangers to the wind-swept fields, the pollen breeze and orchid scent
Stripped of the speech of gurgling streams, bickering birds and pounding rain
Miles below the subtleties and pleasures of a rural Eden

A mockery of the wild horse's spacious and unfettered range
Daunting in its bold dimensions, deep and dark instead of wide
Humid like a bottled storm, precluding that which reeks of death
A death that guards decaying structures built by men who fell in progress

Pausing on a torch-lit step, I close my eyes and concentrate
On distant comely woodland vistas stolen from some antique painting
Cardinals yield a flash of red, flamboyant over virgin snow
A glimpse of evanescent mildness missed as though a mother's face

Another breath resumes the trek through a transromantic underworld
Further down a flickering stairwell plagued with crudely hinting symbols
Travelers reap no sane rewards from such a bleak nocturnal outing
What impending natural force allures me from the sun's caress?

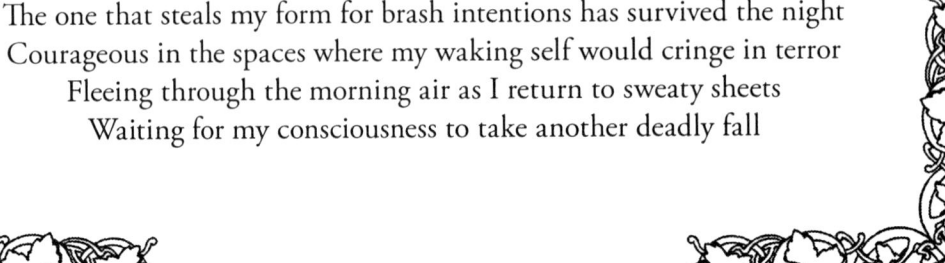

The one that steals my form for brash intentions has survived the night
Courageous in the spaces where my waking self would cringe in terror
Fleeing through the morning air as I return to sweaty sheets
Waiting for my consciousness to take another deadly fall

Away

I know the forces argue but I feel that I deserve a lift
Ready to escape this farce and merge into the sunset cliffs
I lend an ear unto the west until the wise man's whispers cease
In search of that elusive source that hums a softly glowing peace

Withered in a land distraught with cold, materialistic things
Thus I feed myself the sadness just to satisfy my pangs
Life is not a friend to me, I long to roam without its brace
Deep into my thoughts I dig, to carry on without a face

Hymns of warm benevolence come croon into my weary ears
Crafted by an unseen choir, perfected over kinder years
To tantalize my drunken senses now that I've laid down my steel
Singing me a soothing hurt that seems no longer quite as real

Distant cousins roaming free, long buried in the ocean deep
I wish that I could follow them and rest where sleeping secrets keep
I belong to earth and sky that bows to no one in its day
Home to not a single quarrel, command, insult, or evil way

My sympathies will never jade, evasive truth I still defend
My kingdom waits for me out there; it's worth the risks that I intend
Freedom lies in non-existence; back into the womb I fall
Maybe oneness isn't really being anything at all....

The cycle

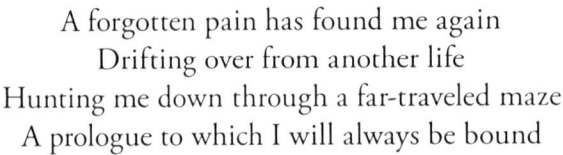

A forgotten pain has found me again
Drifting over from another life
Hunting me down through a far-traveled maze
A prologue to which I will always be bound

Sentiments squirm beneath the ice
Electrified and aglow with strife
Calling my name like a child in need
Making their nest at the back of my mind

I find myself searching familiar terrain
Sucking the dry pipe for inspiration
Timid to turn to those deadly emotions
Each one hot to the amateur's touch

So I crawl inside of a sedative song
Pushing away from the voices of others
Fighting to keep my hungry eyes inward
Melancholic intentions withstanding

Lady luck finds me stubborn to teach
Arguing with my addiction to misery
She dusts me off and directs my gaze
To a trove of undiscovered possessions

Numbered moments then guide my rebirth
As I drink from the fountain of unbridled fortune
Free to explore the most heavenly pinnacles
Deaf to the hiss of a dwindling fuse

Just over hill… a new life, a new love
Waiting for me on a ship of redemption
Ready to sail into unspoken luxury
Leaving the dock as I fall far behind

A faithful return to old, jaded feelings
Tails my new brush with irrational fame
They welcome me home like a manifest sibling
The uglier twin that I left in the dark

A fragment of what I can still never have
Clenched in my hand as a mere souvenir,
I walk yet again down that tired old road
Renewed in the role I had pitied before

A storybook moral with jagged blade edges
Stings and then numbs, like ice to a wound
Release from the astigmatism of bliss
A lesson as rich as the joy once pursued

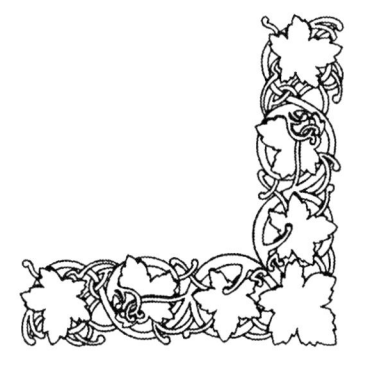

Alignment

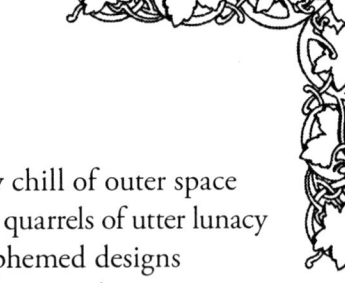

From the earthly warmth of human love to the empty chill of outer space
From the soundest depths of spoken wisdom to the blatant quarrels of utter lunacy
Powers summoned from afar conjugate into blasphemed designs
Writhing to a convincing tune terminated by master alone

A blend of feline-honed finesse and effervescent eagle pride
Trains a sacred art in ways derived from spirit-minded culture
Icons raised from Indian legends ride the crests of ancient pharaohs
Led by graceful animal gods freed from the cage of musing myth

Science and religion breathe enduring life into their child
A pact as old as time itself solidified to spur creation
Twilight rituals open passage, windows to divine commotion
Fallacies of disconnection thaw to show commingled roots

Visions old and new unite to paint an ever-fluxing landscape
Home to alter egos drawn with grains of introspective sands
Beings brought from meditative outings spread eccentric praises
Flowing in a sleek parade of shapely forms unknown to boredom

Sultans of a stranger day return to claim their rightful tiers
Wrapped in oriental fabrics reminiscent of their worlds
Sorcerers resume their sagas, reaching out to swirling skies
A legendary love affair between a wizard and the wild

The age of reason flickers dimly, sucked into an anxious past
Harmony and chaos swapping kisses in a lustrous tangle
Stalkers of a chosen night revel into an equinox
Transcending tired experience with symptoms born of pure volition

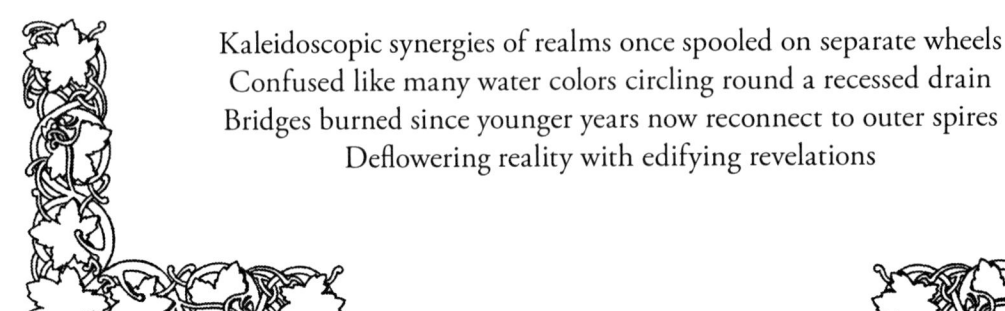

Kaleidoscopic synergies of realms once spooled on separate wheels
Confused like many water colors circling round a recessed drain
Bridges burned since younger years now reconnect to outer spires
Deflowering reality with edifying revelations

Infitialis

Here it comes again, that vaguely sugar spiked acerbic taste
A bittersweet buffet laid out before me; pleasures laid to waste
The same old story plays again, I'm signed up for the same old part
Rejection brings immortal doubt, inherent demons milk my heart

Corrupted by a pretty face; another lesson learned in vain
I'm called out from the royal stock, identified through mortal pain
I've climbed the highest mountainside, determined just to make a stand
Only to discover that my trophy was a barren land

Standards crumble from above, remind me what I'm made out of
I tangle with my petty goals while others are out making love
I've paid my dues a thousandfold, I'm lucky that I'm not so bold
So many times I've lied to say "I'll take my life 'fore I grow old"

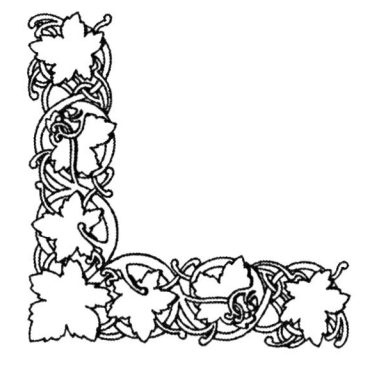

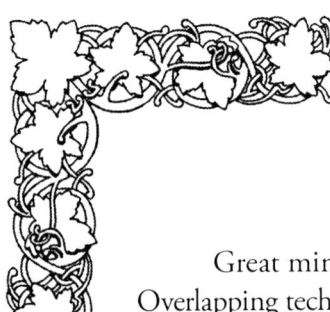

Skyward

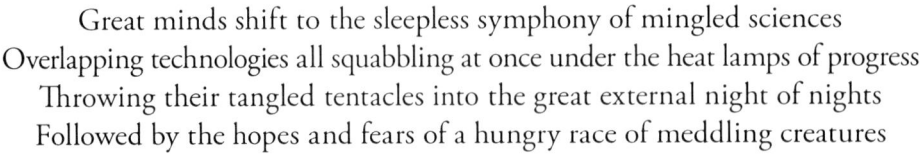

Great minds shift to the sleepless symphony of mingled sciences
Overlapping technologies all squabbling at once under the heat lamps of progress
Throwing their tangled tentacles into the great external night of nights
Followed by the hopes and fears of a hungry race of meddling creatures

Trained to tilt their fierce desires toward horizons lit beyond the heavens,
They strain to look into the clouds with a diligence only the gods could mock
Doors unlocked from years of tampering swing wide open to their gaze
Anomalies once quarantined from sight ride through on capricious winds

Our wildest fantasies elope with our everyday experiences
Spilling from the cracked fist of normalcy into a pit of possibilities
Warmed by the reach of distant cosmic fires safe in their ambiguous niches
Where tireless stars service ruthless planets at the apex of imagination

Genes are poked and prodded while promising potions bubble and froth
Enveloping those that hunch over them in a mystifying cloud of accomplishment
Miracles flooded out of their dark alcoves, rescued from the irony of oblivion
Worn like jewels around the necks of those that shelter a budding revolution

Under the raw assumption that knowledge has agreed to be our servant,
We rise above our animal ignorance to behold the shadows of our efforts
Each time sending our scouts a little farther into the opulence of uncertainty
Retrieving random pieces of a puzzle we may never live to see completed

Weaned on nature's usual milk but raised by the cold hand of industry,
Men of knowledge send forth an army of dangerously imaginative requests
Directing feeble beacons of light across the great ocean of unmeasured awe
Rabid for a religion that beckons from a beautifully austere embrace

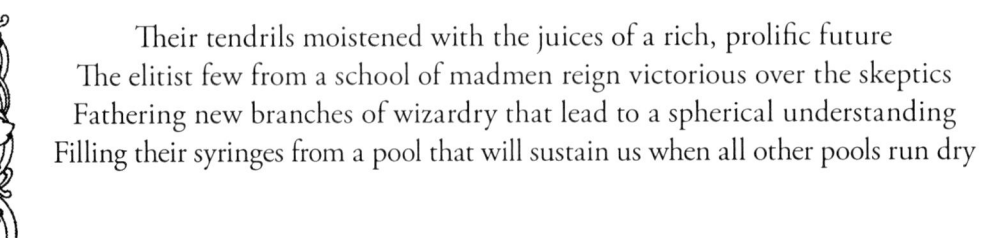

Their tendrils moistened with the juices of a rich, prolific future
The elitist few from a school of madmen reign victorious over the skeptics
Fathering new branches of wizardry that lead to a spherical understanding
Filling their syringes from a pool that will sustain us when all other pools run dry

Odd folk

Strange people need strange things to get them through most every day
They cower in their opium dens and dream their fragile lives away
I, too, tend to dream too much, though I've wandered from that fatal crop
I've gazed through that extrinsic eye, though I knew it all would have to stop

My madness is of natural essence; thoughts for me don't come in tubes
I keep one foot inside the door though I strive to think outside the cube
The tracks that I have left behind have walked the halls of decadence
So don't mistake me for a novice who hasn't been outside the fence

Odd folk such as you and I don't reach fulfillment easily
But we must take caution and not taste the fruit of banished trees
Come full circle and you'll find that treasures hide in closer quarters
Lands beset in milder magic, guarded by more humble porters

Risks are taken lightly by the ones who stray from angel's care
Those who live to self-destruct are keen to feed their own despair
Wholeness is a compromise endeared by convoluted souls
Men would give their prized possessions just to meet their daily tolls

Dementia takes many forms to stalk the steel blue streets at night
Wrapping round a broken man who trembles to an unseen fright
Rags to riches now reversed, he is hollowed by a single flaw
Left to fade in urban pictures tainted with the common law

Your voices are not all ignored, so creep out from your hellish alley
Take a breath of wholesome air before your final days are tallied
Rise to watch your tunneled sight grow brighter with each grain expelled
Take a step outside your mind and the pieces of your lives will meld

The final stretch

I look for the day when the chains will be broken
My wings will unfold and be mended again
No longer to bend to the wrath of compulsion
My crudeness replaced with empowering tools

When I'll learn to outgrow this obtuse asymbolia
The dishonored shepherd that led me astray
A message in nature now lost in translation
Misleads to dark forests of arcane illusion

I preach of the power I call synesthesia
Its succulent aura my ultimate goal
Its pious plasticity slips through my fingers
So faint to my touch yet so close in my mind

The struggle to realize ethereal joys
Has turned my whole life to aesthetic cliché
Only so much can be written of this
For words will soon fail me in capturing anguish

I'm pleased to adhere to the passage of time
The years flow by with a fervent fluidity
Old age will bring me a fresh kind of zen
Removing my thoughts from the turmoil of youth

A natural death waits at the tip of longevity
A tender reply to the blindness of birth
Until then I find ways to keep myself sated
And chew the enigmas that govern my days

I dream of a final binge for answers
The missing components to lifelong dilemmas
Though many partake of my trust in transcendence,
I call for enlightenment brighter than most

When the bell tolls I'll be ready and willing
To unbolt the chambers of sought information
I keep my fate simple and cling to my visions
A light load to carry to grave and beyond

Brandon Gene Petit

At an end

Time has been both cruel and kind
So throw the ashes, pour some wine
Drink, my friend, inhale the brew
For don't you see we've made it through?

And though we're nearly rendered mad
From all those pleasant trips we've had,
The meanings kept are far from wasted
From those ventures that we've tasted

Care to dance? Then choose your girl
And let this grateful night unfurl
The one that has the longest hair,
The greenest eyes and deepest stare

Then let the music take your hand
And lead you to a greater land
Where all's forgotten but not lost
Our stories etched in ageless frost

May there be ten journeys more
All more different than before
Feed your would-be hero make
By going wherever the river may take

Evil drowns amidst our laughter
Hail the days of ever after
Seize the hour while we're young
Our burdens left where coats are hung

We pass the torch to our better halves
And sell our souls to a nobler craft
A toast to all that's gone and done
As well as what has not begun

LaVergne, TN USA
08 September 2010

196260LV00001B/24/A